Stanley Gibbons Collectors Guide

WRITTEN BY **JAMES WATSON**
PRODUCED BY **RUSSELL BENNETT**

STANLEY GIBBONS PUBLICATIONS LTD

391 Strand, London WC2R 0LX

ROYAL WEDDING EDITION

ISBN 0 85259 660 0

Printed in Great Britain by Jarrold & Sons Ltd, Norwich

CONTENTS

INTRODUCTION

The issue of attractive British and Commonwealth postage stamps to commemorate the marriage of H.R.H. Princess Anne to Captain Mark Phillips may have been *your* introduction to the absorbing and rewarding pastime of stamp collecting. If so, then this new Collectors Guide will help you to obtain the greatest enjoyment in pursuit of your newly discovered hobby.

To the philatelist, the world is his oyster, one which can be prised open to reveal an Aladdin's cave of colourful treasure – tens of thousands of stamps from every country you can think of, and more from other places that you may have never even heard of before.

Gibbons's Collectors Guide has been adapted to modern trends in the world's most popular hobby – it is in two parts. Phase 1 deals with the mechanics of getting started, summarised under 'Fundamentals'. Phase 2 develops the theme and introduces the reader to a whole new world of collecting – the pleasures of Philately, which is simply another name for the study of stamps. Only by learning all about them, how they are printed, distributed and used, can you hope to recognise the good and scarce ones, and build up a worthwhile and, maybe, valuable collection.

There is also a short section on Notaphily, the comparatively new banknote hobby, and coins. Currency has strong links with philately and stamps – both have 'face' values – and many collectors combine these interests.

J.W.

PHASE ONE

First Steps – the Fundamentals

This is a kind of ABC of stamp collecting: it assumes that you know little or nothing about stamps, but that you are eager to start on the right lines. Many people begin their collections in a haphazard fashion, spending money on stamps, albums and accessories which eventually prove to be totally unsuitable when the need arises (as it inevitably will) to limit one's scope. It's rather like building a garage before you've decided on the shape and size of a new car! By all means buy a 'stamp collector's outfit' and a monster packet of stamps just to get the 'feel' of collecting, but if you *can* select a certain 'line of country' *before* you have accumulated something of everything, it will be very much to your advantage.

This Guide should help you to make your choice – it emphasises the 'fun' in the fundamentals and outlines the basic essentials for the novice. It is instructive rather than dogmatic: the only rules in stamp collecting are those that you form for yourself, and that is the key to the many hours of enjoyment and relaxation which could be in store for you!

A. Acquiring Stamps – Sources of Supply

To collect unused or postally used stamps? That should be your first consideration. Literally millions of postage stamps are sold by post offices throughout the world every day: millions more are used in the post, so that generally there is no shortage of stamps to choose from. It follows that unused stamps have to be bought, postmarked stamps may be obtained from the mails – friends' letters and business correspondence from abroad. It is not usual to collect both unused *and* used stamps, so let us weigh the pros and cons.

Unused stamps ('mint' if they are in the pristine condition that one expects to buy them at the post office) are generally favoured by the collector who is attracted by the designs on the stamps. Many stamps are miniature works of art and superb examples of the printer's craft, so from that point of view the postmark is a blemish. If, later on, you decide to collect 'thematic' issues – stamps with designs depicting a specific theme or subject such as animals, flowers or sport – then your preference will obviously be for the unused stamps.

New stamps are issued by the countries of the world at the enormous rate of about 6,000 each year (a good reason for being selective!), and most of them – British Commonwealth and foreign – can be purchased from the stamp shop or mail-order dealer

who advertises them in the stamp magazines. Some firms operate 'new issue services' which cater for the regular buyer of new stamps.

British stamps which are in current use (i.e. not obsolete or out of date) can usually be obtained from your local post office. 'Usually' because, while the everyday 'definitive' or ordinary postage stamps are always on hand, the commemorative or 'special' issues such as those for the Royal Wedding this year remain on sale only for limited periods of a few months.

Many collectors prefer stamps which have been used in the post, those which have served their useful purpose and which have perhaps travelled half-way round the world on a letter. To them, the postmark is of major interest – a light cancellation is desirable for a 'fine used' stamp, while the postmark itself may be unusual and attractive (in which case it is sometimes preserved on the envelope). Later on, we will be discussing how to remove used stamps from letters without damaging them.

There are numerous other ways of acquiring stamps. Some dealers sell packets and mixtures – the packets are either of mixed stamps of the whole world, unused and used, or selections of one country or group of countries, while mixtures are just as described, assorted stamps usually on the original pieces of envelope-paper and sometimes sold by weight. The packets mostly contain common stamps, i.e. those in plentiful supply, either unused low values or similar used stamps from the great bulk of the world's mail, and their prices are governed by the cost, not only of the stamps, but of the labour in sorting and classifying them and preparing the packets for sale. Most packets sold by reputable dealers are good value for money.

Among other services provided by the stamp dealer are the sale of stamps 'on approval' and of mixed lots or collections. Many dealers run approval services and send regular selections of stamps, individually priced in booklets, from which the collector can choose the stamps he requires at leisure (though there is usually a time-limit of, say fourteen days or a month, by mutual arrangement). A remittance for the stamps kept is enclosed when the stamps are returned, when the dealer may send another selection suited to the collector's requirements.

Dealers are always buying collections of various kinds and one can buy second-hand ones in the stamp shops. Often the best source for discarded collections and mixed lots of stamps is the auction-room. Study the catalogue, mark the lots that interest you with the prices you are prepared to pay, then

Unused . . .

. . . and fine used

Interesting postal markings

make your bids. You may be lucky, you may not, but it's all part of the excitement in the friendly atmosphere of the auction room. You might acquire an old collection which could be the nucleus of your own potential one, to be rearranged and deployed in a new album.

As soon as you start accumulating stamps, you will want some kind of collecting-book – not necessarily an album – to keep them safely: the answer is a stock-book or album with numerous strips or 'pockets' on a page which will hold all your loose stamps until you have found a permanent home for them. And don't forget that stamps are fragile pieces of paper which require great care in handling. Always use stamp tweezers, then you can call yourself a philatelist!

. . . you will want some kind of collecting book

B. The Catalogue and Other Equipment

Invariably described as the 'stamp collector's Bible', the stamp catalogue is a most essential book of reference. It provides complete, detailed lists of all the stamps issued by a country from the earliest days, with information about dates, reasons for issue, designs, colours, face values and – most important – the current prices (if it is a fairly new catalogue) of the stamps, unused and used. Thousands of stamp illustrations are included to assist the collector in identifying stamps and their country sources.

For the beginner and average collector, the most useful catalogue is *Stamps of the World* which, published annually, records in simplified form, without paper and perforations, watermarks or varieties, all the stamps issued by every country in the world, in alphabetical order. It is one of the most popular catalogues published by Stanley Gibbons, and the only 'whole world' catalogue in this country.

There is, however, a range of other Gibbons's catalogues which may be more applicable to your collecting interests. For the collectors of 'G.B.' (Great Britain) and the British Commonwealth territories, there are two principal ones – the *British Commonwealth Catalogue*, which includes all British and Colonial stamps from the earliest issues to the present time, and the *Elizabethan* which, as its name implies, deals exclusively with the stamps of the present reign for all territories within the Commonwealth, and which also includes details of several thousand errors and varieties.

For the lively G.B./Channel Islands' collector who likes to keep 'on the ball' with constantly changing stamp prices, Gibbons also publish at regular intervals two inexpensive booklets or checklists, *Collect British Stamps* and *Collect Channel Islands' Stamps*. Both editions record the basic stamp issues with their

latest prices, and the stamp illustrations are produced in actual colours.

European countries are catered for in the *Europe 1, 2* and *3 Catalogues* (in three separate volumes arranged in alphabetical order), while the first of the new four-volume series dealing with the countries of Africa, Asia and America – *Overseas 1* – has just been published. All these catalogues are indispensable works of reference for the collector with special interests.

You won't be thinking about becoming a specialist just yet: that requires a long experience and certain skills as explained later in this Guide, but it is as well to know that Gibbons also publish a *Specialised Great Britain Stamp Catalogue* in three volumes – *1. Queen Victoria*; *2. King Edward VII to King George VI*; and *3. Queen Elizabeth*. These record in great detail a wealth of information about the printing and production of British stamps from the Penny Black on.

Most stamp dealers stock Gibbons's catalogues, but if you want a 'preview' why not visit your local public library? Many libraries have a complete range of catalogues and other stamp books. But remember that a stamp catalogue should come high, if not at the top, of your list of 'priorities'.

Stamp tweezers, already mentioned, are another essential item of equipment. Your hands are inevitably moist and constant handling with the fingers tends to spoil stamps – just look at the jacket of a well-thumbed book! With a little practice, tweezers are easy to handle and you wouldn't want to be a 'butter-fingers', would you? They are ideal for sorting stamps and slipping them into that collecting-book you should have purchased by now. Get the tweezer habit!

Some stamp-collector's accessories appear at first to be more suited to engineers or draughtsmen. For example, the perforation gauge. Perforations are a stamp's 'teeth' and they have various measurements (as explained in 'Perforations and Watermarks') which can be ascertained by using a kind of slide-rule gauge, called the 'Instanta'. Other types of perforation gauge have the various measurements, in lines of appropriately sized dots, printed or engraved on card or plastic.

There is another plastic/transparent type of gauge called the Thirkell Position-finder. It has an imprinted grid of small squares (graph or *quadrillé* pattern) with which one can chart or 'plot' the position of stamp flaws and varieties. The squares are numbered across the top and lettered down one side, thus the position 'A1' would indicate a flaw in the top left corner of the stamp.

The detection of watermarks is often a tricky busi-

Measuring a perforation with the 'Instanta' gauge

ness, but, like perforations, sometimes necessary to establish a stamp's designation and value. The watermark is a 'thinned' pattern in the paper, not always apparent, and there are various ways of overcoming its apparent reluctance to reveal itself. One of these is the combination of watermark tray and detector: the latter is simply a small benzine-dropper with a screw-top.

A few drops of benzine (which, note, is highly inflammable) permitted to fall on the stamp, face down in the tray, should reveal the watermark pattern momentarily. There is also a battery-operated instrument known as the 'Philatector' which is an effective aid to watermark detection – the stamps are placed in slides and illuminated through colour filters matching (and 'neutralising') the stamp colours, thus helping to reveal the watermark.

The one 'tool' which everyone, collector or not, associates with the hobby is the magnifying glass. 'The philatelist' is invariably pictured holding a magnifier in the time-honoured style or fashion of Sherlock Holmes! Nevertheless, it is one of the most useful (and most used) accessories in the collector's kit. They range in price according to quality and magnification, needless to say the more you pay the better instrument you get. For the super philatelist there is a precision-made, illuminated magnifier with first-class lenses and variable magnification up to ×7 which is perhaps the ultimate in scientific philately.

You never know when you may need a good glass – at home or 'on location' – so the ideal solution is a good reading-glass for your study or den, and a pocket magnifier to carry around.

The colours of stamps are extraordinarily difficult for some collectors (and experts, too!) to name and classify. In the *Stamps of the World Catalogue*, the naming of colours is kept basically simple – blue, green, red, etc. – but, as you progress with your collection and start using the more detailed catalogues, you may have to select one of six or more colours or shades of what appears to you as just a blue, green or red stamp! To assist you in identifying 'carmine-red' or 'purple-brown', Gibbons have produced a Colour Guide, containing small samples of the 100 colours most used in stamp identification, and a novel Colour Key with pivoting tabs which open out like a fan, displaying 200 colours, including those contained in the aforementioned Guide.

Stamp hinges or mounts are the traditional method of arranging stamps in the album – small rectangles of near-transparent paper, gummed on one side, which are attached to the back of the stamp (near the top)

The 'Philatector'

and then to the album page. If lightly applied, most brands are peelable and one can buy hinges already folded. A modern development is the strip mount, a kind of open-sided envelope or pocket with a gummed back which one sticks to the page. The strips, notably Hawid or Showgard, can be bought in actual strips or cut to stamp size.

Hobby books make essential reading for the enthusiastic collector. Among the best of them is Stanley Phillips's *Stamp Collecting*, available in hardbound and paperback form. *Stamps For All* is a useful little step-by-step family guide for beginners, and *Philatelic Terms Illustrated* is a combined philatelic dictionary and reference book of 192 pages with many full colour plates, explaining all the unusual terms and expressions you are likely to encounter.

Albums come in a later section of this Guide. First we must decide exactly what we are going to collect – for that will influence our choice of album!

C. Your Choice – the One-country Collection

That oyster we mentioned in the Introduction contains about 300 countries of the world which currently issue stamps. This does not include former colonies and provinces, such as New South Wales and Victoria in Australia, and Newfoundland and Nova Scotia in Canada, which at one time issued their own stamps until they were amalgamated into larger states.

In Britain it has been estimated that 4 per cent of the total population, or about 2 million people, actively collect stamps, and that more than half of that number collect 'G.B.', either exclusively or together with the stamps of other countries or groups. So, whatever you decide to collect, you won't be 'going it alone'! At least you will be able to find someone to swap duplicates with.

But perhaps we are 'jumping the starter's pistol' a little. You may have started with that monster packet of stamps and a world album: you may even still be sorting out your stamps into different countries in alphabetical order, and that is the best way of getting to know them and identify them. This is the phase in stamp collecting – mounting one's first stamps in the album under their respective country headings – which experienced philatelists look back on with nostalgia. No complications. Your French stamps belong to the page headed 'France': the German ones – you've guessed 'Deutsche Bundespost' correctly – go under 'German Federal Republic'.

Sooner or later, however, you will feel the urge to confine your collecting to the stamps of certain

Using protective mounts

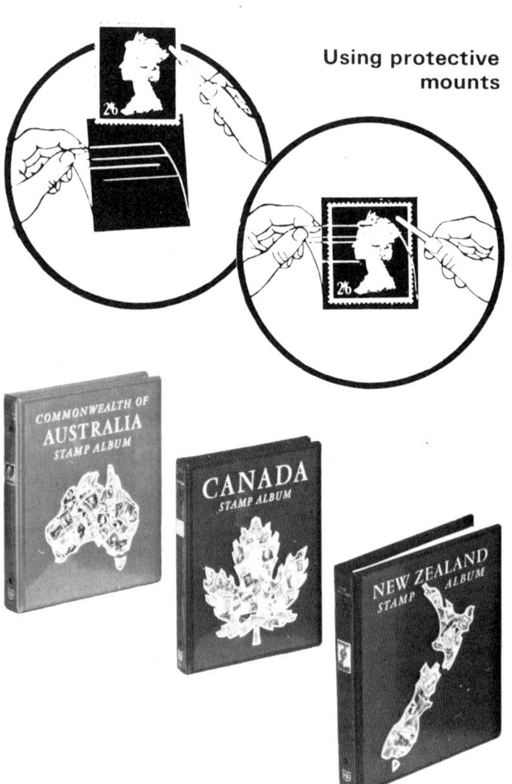

countries, those which attract you more than others, or to particular subjects in stamp designs – anything from butterflies to railway trains. It is a natural instinct to collect the stamps of one's own country or of the country one is living in. The main reason is that these stamps are easily obtained and the collector is 'on hand' when new stamps are issued.

The spark which kindles the urge in a potential 'G.B.' collector is usually a particular commemorative issue, such as those released by the Post Office at the rate of from about six to nine issues each year. The 'Silver Wedding' stamps of 1972 started many people collecting British stamps, as also will the 'Royal Wedding' stamps of 1973. The recent 'Cricket' stamps depicting portly W. G. Grace aroused great interest and were an incentive to collectors to seek other cricket stamps, several of which have been issued in the (British) West Indies.

Most collectors start with the modern issues and develop their collections by working backwards through the reigns. It's far better to keep a weather eye on *all* British stamps – start with a Penny Black of 1840 and build up your collection with representative stamps of Queen Victoria, the four Kings: Edward VII, George V, Edward VIII and George VI, and finally Queen Elizabeth II.

The early Victorian stamps were beautifully engraved and are not quite as dull and unattractive as some collectors imagine them to be. The Penny Blacks and Twopence Blues were followed by the Penny Reds (because the black Maltese Cross postmarks did not show up on the black stamps): the Reds are interesting because they have different 'plate numbers' within their frames, and these are collectable. From 1855, Victorian stamps were 'surface-printed' and there were numerous issues, all bearing the same head of the Queen but in a variety of different colours and settings, until the turn of the century, including the well-known Penny Lilac and the very attractive bicoloured 'Jubilee' issues of 1887–92.

The stamps of Edward VII and George V are keenly sought by collectors. During the latter's reign, Britain's first commemoratives – the 'Wembley' stamps – were issued, while the four stamps for Edward VIII are an interesting souvenir of his short reign. The regular issue of commemorative stamps for special events came into full swing during George VI's reign.

Those who started collecting Elizabethan stamps at the commencement of the Queen's reign in 1952, and who have kept their collections up to date with all the subsequent issues are now 'sitting pretty'. Some 400 British stamps, definitive and commemorative, have

Stanley Gibbons Great Britain Album

been issued during the past twenty years, and many of the earlier stamps have increased in price. It is still possible, nevertheless, to build up an Elizabethan collection by gradual stages.

Other popular 'one-country' subjects are found in Europe and in the Commonwealth territories and foreign states in Africa and Asia, or in the Americas and the West Indies. It really is more adventurous to select just one overseas country, study its people, customs and postal history and then start collecting its stamps. Many would-be collectors are attracted to the beautifully printed stamps of Austria, France, Germany and, especially, Switzerland. Others find satisfaction in the larger Commonwealth territories of Australia, Canada, India and New Zealand, where there is more scope for the ambitious collector.

Islands are popular – that is why so many collectors are turning to the Channel Islands, Jersey and Guernsey, and to the Isle of Man (which now has its own postal administration and stamps, in the wake of Jersey and Guernsey), or even further afield to the 'paradise' islands of Barbados, Bermuda, Jamaica and the Bahamas. South Pacific islands like Pitcairn, Fiji and the Gilbert and Ellice groups or remote outposts such as Ascension and Tristan da Cunha in the Atlantic all have their philatelic supporters.

The 'one-country' man (or woman) is able to concentrate on his or her chosen country or group to the exclusion of all other stamps: all one's finances, too, can be directed towards the ultimate goal of a reasonably complete collection of the country's stamps, earlies and moderns, postal history items and postmarks, and the purchase of catalogues, handbooks and albums. It's great fun 'adopting' a faraway country!

D. Your Choice – the Thematic Collection

Some stamp designs *were* dull and unimaginative during the last century. Excessively formal portraits of the reigning monarch, or some equally uninspiring symbolic emblems, were the order of the day. Gradually, all this changed and the various countries of the world began competing with one another in the production of more and more pictorial stamps depicting every subject under the sun.

Staid portraits of presidents and national heroes, historic battles and public buildings issued in the 1920s and 1930s were replaced by bigger, brighter and (alleged) 'better' stamps depicting the things that most postal administrations imagined (with an eye to revenue) the collector wanted – wild animals,

exotically coloured birds, flowers, ships, the Olympic Games, aircraft, scouting, jazz musicians, spacecraft, famous paintings and the local Cola factory . . . the list is unending.

As everyone knows (or soon finds out) very many countries, notably some of the Arab Gulf states and Latin-American republics, have been overdoing it with the result that their steady streams of colourful labels (which is all some of them are) have been boycotted by the very people who would normally have collected them.

Despite this, the picture on the stamp is the principal attraction for many collectors, especially the designs which tie in with another interest, possibly naval vessels, bird-watching, painting or horticulture. The attraction of thematic collecting – the pursuit of a certain 'theme' or subject – is that the collector becomes very much of an individualist.

His pleasure is in tracking down all or any of the stamps depicting his chosen subject – cats or composers, doggies or dandelions (see Switzerland, S.G. J183!). The more remote and outlandish the subject, the more exciting is the chase, plus the extreme pleasure of finding new stamps which 'fit in' to a particular narrative or story.

For thematic collecting has developed beyond the mere accumulation of famous people or fishes, with perhaps page after page of assorted fruits or fungi. There has to be some semblance of order in the collection: at the very least a grouping of 'types' together (with some appropriate written notes). Reptiles, for example, are a fascinating group among the cold-blooded vertebrates: the class includes lizards, snakes, alligators and crocodiles, and you would surely keep them well apart from each other (even on the album page!).

You would – should – assemble your crocs under the Order Crocodilia; chameleons, iguanas and most of the lizards (in their respective families) under Squamata; and snakes, of which there are three main divisions or families – pythons and boas; cobras, mambas and snakes various; and adders and vipers, under the suborder Ophidia. All animal life – the Primates (monkeys and apes); Carnivora (cats, dogs, bears etc.); Rodentia (gnawing animals); and Ungulata (hoofed animals), can be assembled in the album on scientific lines, grouped in orders and families.

An alternative arrangement would be to group the mammals and reptiles under the continents, subdivided into countries, where they are found, a geographical arrangement rather than the formal scientific

one. It all depends whether you have leanings towards world travel or zoology!

Most thematic subjects can be tackled along the same lines. 'Architecture' could show modern buildings stemming from the long sequence of Ancient Egyptian, Greek, Roman, Byzantine, and Gothic styles. Astronomy is a subject as vast as the Universe itself and is linked with modern developments in space travel. Music is a theme with many variations – opera, ballet, the classics, composers and instruments. Transport, another vast topic, embraces motor-cars, aircraft, railways and ships . . . it's *your* choice!

Based on the maxim that 'every picture tells a story', the narrative or story form of thematic collecting makes use of stamps as a kind of picture-story with a beginning and an end. It could be the life of some famous person, supported by stamps depicting not only the V.I.P. himself at various periods of his life, but depicting all the events with which he was connected – parliamentary affairs, wars and battles, revolutions, accomplishments and, utter finality, death.

On stamps one can trace the lives of the great explorers – Columbus, Captain Cook, Stanley and Livingstone; famous statesmen – Sir Winston Churchill being first choice; the great masters of music – Bach, Beethoven, Handel, Mozart and many more; famous men of science like Copernicus or Leonardo da Vinci.

On quite another tack, the story-line could relate to the growth and development of a specific country, one with a colourful history – Switzerland and the formation of the cantons; Malta and the Knights of the Order of St John, the Great Siege and the events which led to the award of the George Cross to the island in 1942; the progress of the Australian States leading to the formation of the Commonwealth of Australia, and of the Canadian provinces up to the Confederation of the Dominion of Canada.

People and places – all have tremendous scope for the thematic story-teller. Yet there is a third approach which may again be subdivided: one theme is the pictorial study of our great religions, e.g. Christianity, and worldwide institutions such as the United Nations and the International Red Cross. Industrial development of such essential commodities as iron and steel, copper and oil, and the great engineering achievements of the past century are themes which readily come to mind.

Once you've chosen your subject, you should then go through your whole-world catalogue, page by page, country by country, listing all the possible stamps. It's well worth the effort!

E. Albums – Arrangement and Layout

First, about stamp albums in general. Whatever you have decided to collect – whole world, one country or theme – there is an album 'tailor-made' to suit your taste, scope and pocket. They are available from your stamp dealer in all shapes and sizes at prices ranging from about 50p for the simple printed album to *x* pounds for the super leather-bound job. Somewhere between these extremes you will find just what you need.

Gibbons publish the widest range – therefore the biggest choice – of albums in this country, so let's look through their publications list. Printed albums, those with printed country headings at the top of each page, include fastbound – Fanfare and Strand also the new Safari – and looseleaf types with springback binders – Swiftsure, Worldex and International. The great advantage of the springback album is, of course, that the leaves can be rearranged at the drop of a hat, and extra leaves may be added as your collection grows.

If you have settled for 'G.B.', then there is a Gibbons 'one-country' album ideal for a simple straightforward collection from 1840 to date (including annual supplements), and a similar volume for the Channel Islands. The Windsor is a handsome album for the G.B. collector. It contains printed spaces for all G.B. stamps with detailed illustrated lists contained in three types of springback binder – Popular, Library and Presentation editions, kept up to date with regular supplements.

Another very popular G.B. album for 'Special Stamps' has the pages laid out to accommodate all the British commemorative and special issues from the 1924 Wembley issues to date, and there are ten other 'one-country' albums for some of the most popular countries and groups as, for example, Australia, New Zealand, Canada, Falkland Islands, The Saints (Kitts, Lucia and Vincent) and Switzerland.

For the 'do-it-yourself' collector who prefers to arrange and 'write up' his collection on blank leaves there are many splendid albums to choose from, priced according to size, capacity and quality with springback, ring-fitting or peg-fitting binders. The most popular springbacks are the Senator Standard and Medium (slightly smaller leaf), Simplex Standard and Medium (bordered 'cream' leaf), also a De-Luxe edition, and the Utile Standard and De Luxe. Utile leaves are double-linen-hinged which means that they lie flat when the album is opened. Stamps show up well on a black background and if you prefer black leaves, then the Nubian springback is the album for you.

The 'Windsor' Album

Gibbons's newest looseleaf multi-ring fitting album is called, appropriately, Ring 22 – it flicks open at a touch and again there is the convenience of the leaves lying flat so that you can work on them in the binder. Medium-priced albums on similar lines are the Abbey and the Albany, the latter having standard-size leaves.

Peg (or 'pillar') fitting albums tend to be square in format because the pegs take up more marginal space. They range from the 200-leaf Wyon and the 250-leaf Devon to the better-quality Exeter and luxury Plymouth, the latter both available with 50 linen-hinged leaves.

How to house your covers

There are no less than four types of album for cover collectors, e.g. first-day covers and airmail flown covers, the Arch, the Pioneer, the Thames and the 'S.G.', while there is also a special booklet album for stamp booklets, and albums for banknotes and coins. Collecting-books, already mentioned, are available in various sizes and qualities, from the pocket-book type to the large 12×9 in. stock-book.

Once you have decided on the *type* of album you require, you should ask your dealer to show you a selection. Many albums are supplied with 'faced' leaves or transparent interleaving; many also are provided with 'slip-in' cases for permanent protection.

Arranging your collection – such as it is – in the album is for most people the most enjoyable and satisfying part of the whole exercise. Confronted with 50 or 100 blank, virgin-white leaves, and with your stamps, tweezers and hinges close at hand, it seems a simple matter just to stick the stamps in 'as they come'. But you must have some semblance of order, chronological or otherwise, and it is as well to plan your layout in advance, before you start licking hinges.

If you have settled on one country, then you will know from the catalogue which stamps you have and which you are missing: you have to decide whether you have a reasonable chance of obtaining the missing ones to fill the gaps which you should, optimistically, leave for them. Try out some preliminary arrangements with the loose stamps, allowing space for intended headings and written notes. Your stamps should be laid out in neat rows, from six to nine in a row depending on the size of the stamps and of the album leaf. Don't cram too many stamps on a page; on the other hand, don't space them out to exaggerated lengths.

How to arrange your collection

The overall appearance of a full page of stamps should be pleasing to the eye and well balanced: vary the number of stamps in a row, with perhaps fewer at the top and bottom to obtain the desired effect. Most blank leaves have a faint *quadrillé* pattern of tiny squares printed on them to enable you to calculate distances and spaces between stamps, which you can plot with light pencil dots. Always aim to have complete issues or sets on a page – it looks so much neater than having 'stragglers' on a following page.

If you have a set of stamps of mixed shape and size, you need not stick to the normal order of face value, but arrange them with an eye to symmetry – horizontal formats in one row, verticals in the adjacent row. Juggle them around a little and you may find a satisfactory combination of both formats, e.g. two vertical stamps flanked by one or two horizontal designs on either side, but always in level rows.

The headings on each page should be uniformly styled: these and any necessary 'writing up' ought to be done *before* you start mounting your stamps. Written notes should be concise and provide just the essential information required, preferably *above* the stamps referred to. If your album is not of the 'lie-flat' type, take the leaves out of the binder to work on them. These principles (rather than 'rules') can be bent a little in the case of a thematic collection where a less rigid arrangement, with more copious notes, may be more desirable.

Hinging stamps is a comparatively simple operation. Just fold down about a quarter of the hinge, gummed side outwards, and lightly moisten the narrow folded part with the tip of your tongue: attach that portion to the back of the stamp a little below the top perforations. Next, moisten the lower part of the 'flap' or lower side of the hinge and attach the entire ensemble of hinged stamp to the album page – in its allotted space – and lightly press down. Practise handling the hinges with your tweezers: you will soon become a skilful mounter-upper! But don't attempt to remove a hinge before it is thoroughly dry: if you do, it will bring away part of the album page (or the stamp) with it.

The procedure for mounting Hawid or Showgard strips is much the same – the strips are ready-gummed and, if cut to the required size, can be mounted in the same neat rows as hinged stamps. They may, however, take up a little more space.

Condition is paramount: never put a damaged stamp in your album, or one with paper attached. Clipped stamps from letters should be 'floated' (rather than soaked) in a basin or tray of lukewarm water for twenty minutes or so, when you will find that they are easily detached from the pieces of paper. Dry them between sheets of clean blotting-paper and then, only then, they are ready for mounting.

Some old stamps are worth more on the original envelope, especially if there are some interesting and

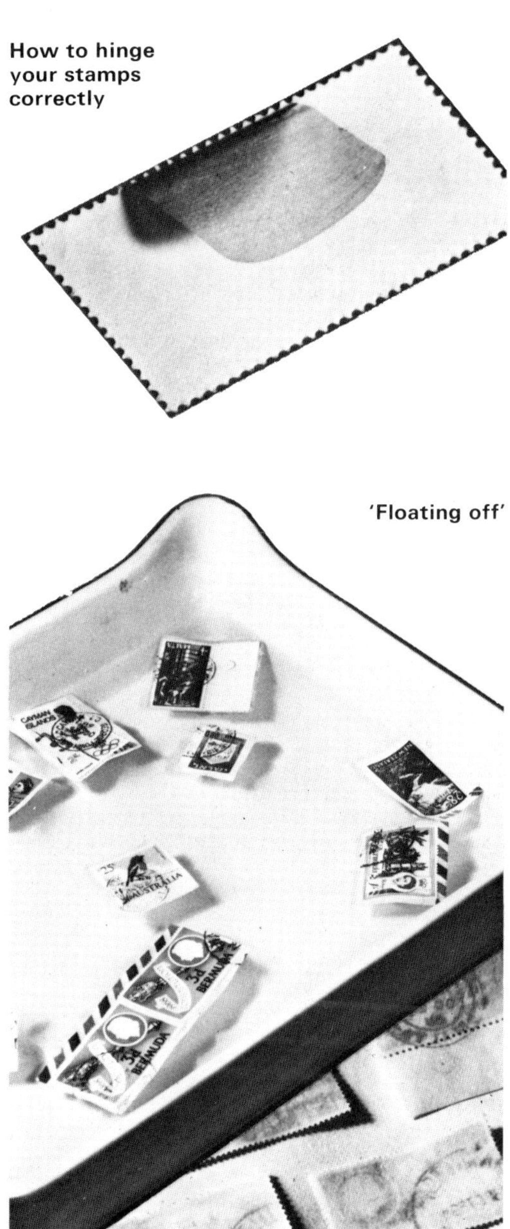

How to hinge your stamps correctly

'Floating off'

unusual postmarks, so think about that before you cut off the stamps!

PHASE TWO

Philately Without Tears

The terms 'stamp collecting' and 'philately' are more or less synonymous, but the true philatelist is an adult student of stamps – their design and manufacture, their history and postal significance. He is usually also a 'specialist' which means, in the strict philatelic sense, that he devotes his studies to the particular issue(s) of a certain country and their printing techniques, to certain aspects of its postal history (including the period before stamps were used) and to anything else, such as postal stationery, etc. which may be relevant.

It follows that a good knowledge of the printing processes employed in the making of postage stamps, of the origin and development of stamps and the postal services, and of the political and social backgrounds of a specific country all contribute to the qualifications of a philatelist. There are many specialised and excellent handbooks for the philatelic student to read: more than likely there is one on your own chosen subject.

Printing, Perforations and Watermarks

First, *kinds* of stamps. Besides the definitive and commemorative stamps which every country issues, there are various other types in general use – official or 'service' issues for government mail; airmail stamps for letters transported exclusively by air; charity stamps, which bear a premium devoted to worthy causes; postage-due stamps used on insufficiently prepaid (or unpaid) letters to indicate the charge collectable; provisionals – stamps overprinted and/or surcharged for emergency use; and the special stamps for various postal services – express, special delivery, parcels, newspapers and registration. Locals, fiscals and telegraph stamps, usually non-postal, are regarded as 'Cinderella' issues, though some people do collect them.

All these stamps are printed by one of four different printing processes, sometimes by a combination of two of them. But first it is the job of the artist or stamp designer to prepare the artwork for the designs, and his presentation will vary according to the printing method used. His source of design may be a photograph or a painting: he has to adapt it to a convenient size and to include the necessary country name, inscriptions, emblems and face value.

The oldest and most highly regarded process of

Official

Express

Postage Due

Special Delivery

Registered

Pneumatic Post

Too Late

Regional

Air Mail

printing is line-engraving or recess, which the printers call 'intaglio' (cut or hollowed out). The old Penny Black was line-engraved and the traditional methods of engraving dies and preparing printing plates is still in use today.

The stamp design is cut or etched by the engraver on a copper or steel die *in reverse*. This master die is hardened and its hollowed or recessed image applied to the softer steel surface of the 'transfer roller', which, when hardened, is used to 'rock in' the design on the steel printing plate as many times as required to form what will be, when printed, a complete sheet of stamps. These are printed either from a flat plate in single sheets, or from a plate which has been curved round a cylinder for continuous printing on a rotary machine. The designs on the printing plate are again in recess and you can feel the raised impression on the printed stamps.

Photogravure printing has been used for stamps since about 1914, and it is another form of recess printing, but instead of being copied by the engraver, the original artwork is photographed and transferred in various stages to be etched on the copper printing cylinder. The stamp image is composed of tiny recesses or 'cells' which vary in depth according to the intensity of colour required on the printed stamps and which appear on them as tiny dots. Multicoloured stamps are printed from several cylinders 'in tandem', one for each colour.

Photo-lithography is the modern version of lithography or 'offset' lithography, a form of surface-printing originally invented in 1796, when the design image was applied by a greased crayon to the flat 'stone' or, if multiple images were required, by 'transfers'. The stone then having been wetted, the printing ink adhered only to the dry image required to be printed. Nowadays, the design is photographed on to a flexible aluminium or zinc plate which is wrapped round a cylinder: a rubber roller transfers or 'offsets' the design to the paper.

Letterpress or 'typography' (which has other meanings) is the normal method of printing from raised type, the oldest known process of printing. For stamp work, the design is engraved in relief, moulds are cast from it and these, after being chemically processed, form a printing plate. Few stamps are embossed these days, but the principle is the bringing together (or 'marriage') of two matching dies, one (male) in relief, the other (female) in recess.

Stamps are perforated usually in single sheets, sometimes in the rotary printing press (which is fed by reels of paper 'in the web') when the perforator is a

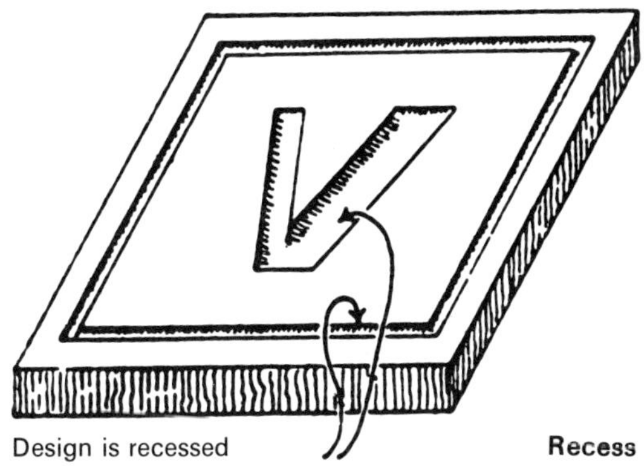

Design is recessed **Recess**

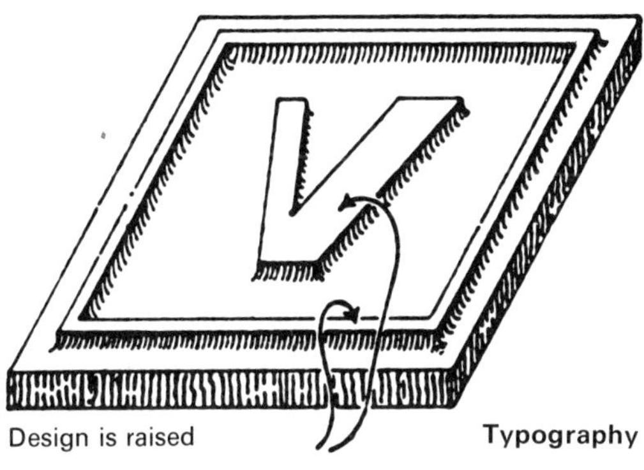

Design is raised **Typography**

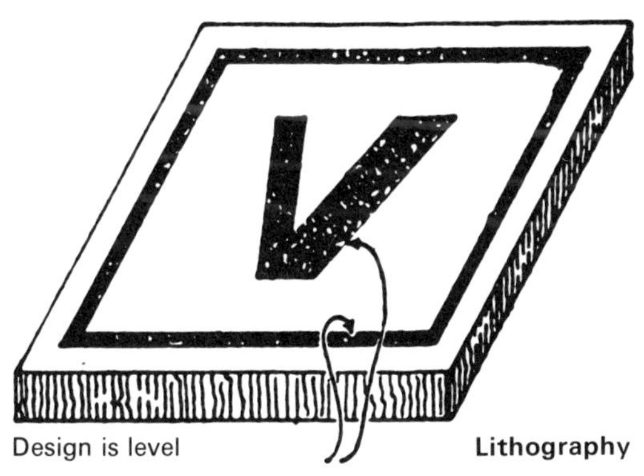

Design is level **Lithography**

part of the integral equipment. Some machines produce single 'line perforations', in others the perforating pins are in the form of a 'comb' which punches several rows, top and sides, at a time. Rouletting is a means of separation in which cuts are made in the paper by a roulette-wheel or toothed disk.

Perforations have different measurements according to the machine used, and these are important in philately as otherwise identical stamps may be reprinted in a different gauge, while also having a shorter life. The 'yardstick' is the number of perforation holes within the measure of 2 centimetres, and these can vary from 7 to about 18. Mixed perforations are shown in the catalogue with the horizontal perf. first, then the vertical measure, e.g. $12\frac{1}{2} \times 14$.

Watermarks are simply distinguishing 'thinned' marks or emblems formed in the paper at the pulp stage, by the 'dandy roll' which has a wire-gauze pattern. Watermarked paper was originally a security precaution, but the practice is falling into disuse. British stamps are no longer watermarked.

A watermark as viewed from the back of the stamp

Errors and Varieties

Everyone is eager to find some flaw or fault in a printed stamp, hoping thereby to make a small fortune when the discovery is revealed to an incredulous world. In most cases one's reward is indeed small, but the excitement persists, the search goes on and occasionally someone finds a sheet of 'missing heads' or one which is imperforate (i.e. without perforations), finding himself several thousand pounds richer as a consequence. It is probably the only pastime in the fields of art, graphic design and printing in which mistakes make money!

There is after all, immense scope for error in all the intricate stages of stamp production. Right at the beginning the designer may make a simple mistake of identity, caption or design. Well-known instances are Columbus using a telescope on a St Kitts-Nevis stamp, Fiji's unmanned canoe in full sail, Jamaica's upside-down Union Jack, the Pitcairn schoolteacher's house labelled 'Pitcairn School', Schubert's music on an East German stamp honouring Schumann and the very numerous mapping errors of latitude and longitude.

Spelling errors are frequent and one remembers 'Wakatipu' appearing as 'Wakitipu' on a New Zealand stamp of 1898, and 'Jesselton' shown as 'Jessleton' on a North Borneo (Sabah) issue. There is a quite famous Greek stamp inscribed 'Sir Codrington', his correct title being 'Sir Edward Codrington', and the equally amusing 'Lord Bacon' for 'Sir Francis Bacon' on a

Newfoundland stamp of 1910. Such errors have no especial value as they occur on every issued stamp.

Often the most spectacular printing errors are the most valuable ones, and one calls to mind India's first stamp, the Queen Victoria 4 annas, with inverted head; the United States 24-cent airmail stamp with the 'Inverted Jenny' aeroplane; and the Canada 'St Lawrence Seaway' stamp with its centre upside-down – all due to the same circumstance, a printing plate for a separate part of the design inserted wrongly in the press.

Europe's rarest stamp, the Sweden 3-skilling-banco, yellow, is an error of colour – it should have been green – while among the most valuable stamps issued by the Cape of Good Hope are the 'Woodblock' errors of colour, 1d blue and 4d vermilion, caused by clichés being switched when the printing plates were being prepared.

Among the best-known watermark errors are the inclusion of a 'Tudor' crown in place of the 'St Edward's' crown in certain British colonial issues of 1950–52, and the Transvaal 1d Edwardian stamp of 1905–09 with the 'Cabled Anchor' watermark of the Cape of Good Hope! Mishaps of perforation are not without interest and these take various forms, stamps being found perforated diagonally or down the centre, partially or entirely imperforate, notably in stamp booklets. Note, however, that booklets are often trimmed close giving straight edges to some of the stamps therein.

The most common errors these days are usually allied to the photogravure-printing process, either missing colours (which means that part of the design is missing as well), or massive shifts of parts of a design which, being separately printed, may be badly misaligned, overlapping another part of the design.

Flaws and varieties are very numerous on modern stamps and the study and collection of them has become a *raison d'être* for many collectors. One can hardly blame the poor printers (not literally 'poor'!) who are called upon to produce millions of stamps every day of the week, at high speed and at full capacity. Generally, printing standards are high.

Photogravure flaws are usually blemishes which appear as deformities in parts of the design or as white patches and spots or misplaced colours. If such varieties occur on the same stamp on every sheet they are regarded as 'constant', which gives them a certain status. Often they are 'retouched' by the printer. 'Doubling' on a line-engraved stamp is caused by 're-entries' when the 'transfer roller' is in operation, and part of a design has to be 'rocked in' again.

Sweden's rare error of colour

Missing Queen's head

Normal (above), missing colour (below)

A massive design shift

Postal History and Postmarks

The history of the postal services is a fascinating subject, one with which most stamp collectors become involved at one stage or another. Postal history, which became a popular and highly specialised collecting hobby on its own merits just a few years ago, is now an established part of the philatelic scene. It is not, as some people imagine, 'all clay tablets and couriers': it is the romantic story of the origin and development of the world's posts, represented by the folded letter-sheets and primitive postal markings of the pre-stamp era, the coming of the Penny Post and of stamps themselves, the establishment of postal rates and charges (both for inland and overseas mails), and the gradual use of packet-ships and aircraft in the transport of the mails.

It was about the year 1516 that Henry VIII, anxious to maintain communications with France and other parts of Britain following the War of the Holy Alliance, appointed Sir Brian Tuke as the first 'Master of the Posts'. Tuke was responsible for stage-'posts' between London and the ports and other towns, but this was an exclusive 'Royal' courier-post: no private letters were permitted to be carried.

Then, in the seventeenth century, the London merchants started their own posts, and in 1661, four years after the revolutionary Post Office Act, one Henry Bishop, who had been appointed 'Postmaster-General' by Charles II, introduced the 'post mark'. Known as 'Bishop marks', these were small, circular handstamps showing the date and the first two letters of the month, and they remained in use until 1787 – the forerunners of the familiar postmark cancellations of the present day.

William Dockwra, a City of London merchant, inaugurated his rival Penny Post in 1680 and introduced the first handstruck 'post paid' stamp – a triangular mark inscribed 'Penny Post Paid'. In later years, penny posts sprang up all over Britain and the various postal markings are avidly collected (on their original letters) and treasured by postal historians.

During the eighteenth century, while the great Thurn and Taxis postal network was operating at its peak throughout Europe, Ralph Allen, the Bath Postmaster, managed the complex system of 'by' and 'cross' (or 'cross-country') posts, resulting in a profusion of distinctive 'town' postmarks on the folded (and wax-sealed) letters and wrappers. Stage coaches were in use, but it was John Palmer, also of Bath, who pioneered the first mail coaches in Britain. Then, from about 1830, mail began to be carried on the newly constructed railways.

Seventeenth-century courier

French letter-carriers

Mail coach

The ports of Britain and the overseas colonies and dominions are favourite stamping-grounds for the postal historian who specialises in the prolific field of eighteenth- and nineteenth-century ship letters and their picturesque markings. Many packet-boats bound for America and the West Indies ran the gauntlet of pirates and buccaneers, while the numerous 'Paquebot' cancellations of more recent times – usually applied aboard the packet-vessels or at the port of arrival – are popular with collectors.

The student/historian is especially interested in the postal rates of a certain country, and in the various combinations of postage stamps required and used to make up these rates. Sometimes additional stamps issued by another country had to be applied to letters to ensure onward transmission – 'combination covers', as they are known, are keenly sought by collectors. The routing of letters, evinced from their postal markings, is of particular interest, as also are the relative post office notices, documents and way-bills.

Soldiers' letters and the transport of the mails in time of war engage the attention of many postal historians – letters from the Crimea and from South Africa during the Boer War are cherished for their varied postal markings, while those used in the two world wars, with their innumerable field post office cancellations and censor marks, are regarded as very desirable collectors' pieces. It becomes increasingly apparent that the postmark, and the story it has to tell, is the key to most aspects of postal history.

The year 1840 saw the introduction of Rowland Hill's Uniform Penny Postage scheme with its 'new-fangled' black and blue postage stamps – the world's first – and the much-maligned Mulready envelopes and covers or wrappers. At the same time, the Maltese Cross handstamp cancellations were brought into use – they were hand-made so that no two are exactly alike. Many distinguishable types were used in London and in other towns and cities in Britain.

These were followed by a succession of cancellation types – post office code numerals within barred circles and ovals (known as 'killers'), combined town datestamp and numerals such as the so-called 'spoons', later in common use as 'duplex' handstamps, the 'sunburst' types used in Scotland and the gradual evolvement of the circular town cancellation in use today.

Postmarks in use at the turn of the century included the attractive 'squared circles', the single-circle c.d.s. or circular datestamp (including the very small 'thimble' marks used mainly on picture postcards in the Edwardian era), the double-circle c.d.s. and other

The Siege of Paris

The Siege of Mafeking

Maltese Cross on Mulready envelope

types. Postmarks of this period are best collected on card or cover, and the scarcest ones are those used in the smaller post offices.

A later development was the machine cancellation, which was speedily adapted to include slogans. These commenced in 1917 with the slogan 'Buy National War Bonds Now' – nowadays virtually every post office has its machine/slogan cancellation. Some of the pictorial ones are very attractive.

British stamps 'used abroad' have a special attraction for some collectors: in the last century, before the Colonies had their own postage stamps, British stamps were used and the postmark is the only means of identifying such usage.

Railway enthusiasts collect the 'Travelling Post Office' ('T.P.O.') and 'Sorting Carriage' postmarks applied to letters posted in mail trains or carried by them.

Rare Stamps and Covers

'Rarity' is defined as 'something valued for its scarcity'. The world's most famous and rare stamps are generally those of which only a few exist, and most of them are well documented and recorded. Occasionally they change hands at ever increasing prices!

The distinction of being the 'rarest stamp in the world' belongs to the British Guiana 1 cent black on magenta of 1856. It was discovered in 1873 by a schoolboy who lived there and soon afterwards he sold it to a local collector. As time passed and it was realised that the stamp was the only one of its kind in existence (it had had little use in the colony), it passed through many hands, finally being sold, in 1970, to an American syndicate for the equivalent of £116,600. When, in 1965, it was displayed at Gibbons Catalogue Centenary Exhibition at the Royal Festival Hall in London, it was insured for £200,000.

Among the best-known rarities are the celebrated Mauritius 'Post Office' stamps of 1847. They were locally engraved and printed in quantities of 500 each of the 1d and 2d – only 14 and 12 respectively have survived and these are now extremely valuable. A unique cover bearing one of each value was sold for £28,000 in 1963, while another envelope franked with two 1d 'Post Office' stamps realised over £150,000 at an auction in 1968. Unused, the 1d and 2d stamps are catalogued at £40,000 each. The finest known example of the 2d unused is now in the Royal Collection.

'Home-made' stamps which became great rarities were those issued by Postmaster W. B. Perot of Hamilton, Bermuda, for some years commencing in

Travelling Post Office cancellations

British Guiana 1c

1d 'Post Office' Mauritius

Bermuda 'Perot'

1848. Customers used to pop letters into his box without the necessary pennies to cover the postage, so he made his own stamps, using his postmark handstamp, dated and initialled, on sheets of paper which he cut up and distributed. Only eleven of the rare 'Perot' stamps have ever come to light – three of them are in the Royal Collection.

There are numerous other rare stamps among the 'classics' of the Commonwealth – the British Guiana 'Cottonreels', Canada's 'Twelvepence' black of 1851 (a beautiful stamp), Trinidad's 'Lady McLeod', some of the Cape Triangulars, and the 'Sydney Views' of New South Wales. Comparatively rare is Britain's Penny Black which, unused, is catalogued from £125 to £200: in blocks or multiples it would be extremely rare. A rare Edwardian is the 2d Tyrian plum (£3,500); others are the 6d purple 'I.R. OFFICIAL' overprinted stamp (£12,000 un.) and the 10s stamp in the same issue (£2,750 un., or with the 'raised stop' variety, £3,000).

Among the rarest European stamps are the cantonal issues of Switzerland – Basel, Geneva and Zürich, issued in 1843–45, while further afield the Brazilian 'Bull's-Eyes' and Hawaiian 'Missionaries', some of them at least, bear the 'rare stamp' cachet.

Rarities in modern issues are usually confined to the more spectacular errors of printing (see 'Errors and Varieties'). In such cases, everyone has the opportunity of discovering them by keeping a watchful eye when purchasing stamps at the post office! A classic instance of that was the sale of $2\frac{1}{2}$d King George V Silver Jubilee stamps in the experimental colour of Prussian blue (instead of blue) by error at a post office in Edmonton, London, in 1935, now £350 unused in the catalogue. Come to think of it, nearly all the great rarities were sold originally 'over the post office counter'.

It is the legendary ambition of every schoolboy to find or to own a great stamp rarity, a worthy ambition but one hardly likely to be realised except in the most fortuitous circumstances. But there are many thousands of 'medium' rarities – those which have a catalogue value upwards of, say, £50 or £100 – which *can* be found through diligent search. How? By study and research and acquiring a good knowledge of stamps in general. Knowing what to look for – in the stamp shop, auction-room, yes, even in the post office, can be the stepping-stone to success.

Stamps for Investment

The collector who studies his stamps and uses the knowledge gained to build up a fine collection, buying

Great Britain 2d 'Tyrian Plum'

U.S.A. 24c Air with inverted centre

Cape of Good Hope 'Woodblock'

Bidding at a stamp auction

(within his means) choice stamps and material for it, has the best of both worlds. Like the gardener who loves flowers and 'watches his garden grow', the philatelist loves stamps, derives pleasure from them and enjoys the gradual process of developing a worthwhile collection.

At the same time, he is building up a good, solid investment for himself – or maybe his heirs – and there's hardly a collector in the land who does not give a thought to the potential value of his collection, and how that value may be enhanced and increased by judicious purchases. That is human nature and the collector knows that if, through some misfortune, he has to dispose of his stamps, he has a reasonable chance of recovering a substantial proportion of his initial outlay, and may even make a profit.

The collector 'most likely to' is the one who has made a specialised collection or study of a selected country or group of countries, or even of certain stamp issues within a country. The enthusiast who forms a collection of G.B. Edwardians, with the printings by De La Rue, Harrison & Sons and Somerset House expertly segregated, with nice unused examples of all the different shades, with some choice post-marked items and covers, and perhaps a range of the postal stationery – stamped postcards, envelopes and wrappers – of the period, is making a wise and secure investment.

For a stamp collection to be 'sale-worthy', however, there are certain criteria. Condition is paramount – the knowledgeable, discerning collector will select only stamps in fine condition, unblemished and undamaged, even replacing slightly inferior copies when he finds better examples. Good planning and neatness in arrangement is certain to give a favourable impression to the prospective buyer. There's a lot to be said for 'window-dressing'!

Successful investment, in stamps as in any other marketable commodity, is not something that can be guaranteed. It depends very largely upon a lively awareness of market trends and a thorough knowledge of the commodity (in our case, stamps) one proposes to invest in.

The broker can only *recommend* which stocks and shares you should buy: the final decision is yours. The stamp dealer can only *advise* you which, in his experience, are the most likely stamps to increase in value. But reputable stamp dealers *are* prepared to recommend and offer short-term or long-term 'portfolios' of stamps (which may be 'gilt-edged' classics or 'blue-chip' modern issues) for investment. In such cases, the dealer is placing his first-hand knowledge

Hawaiian 'Missionaries'

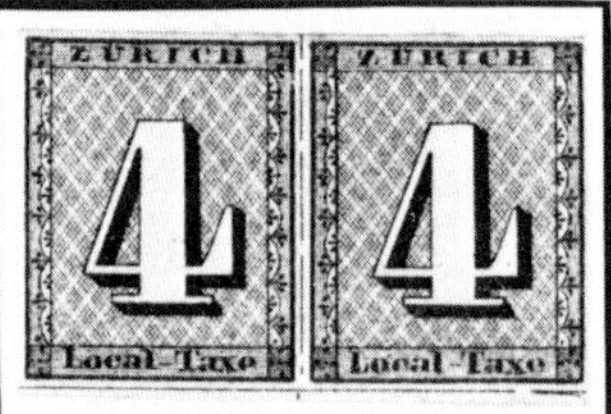

Zurich

. . . build up a fine collection . . .

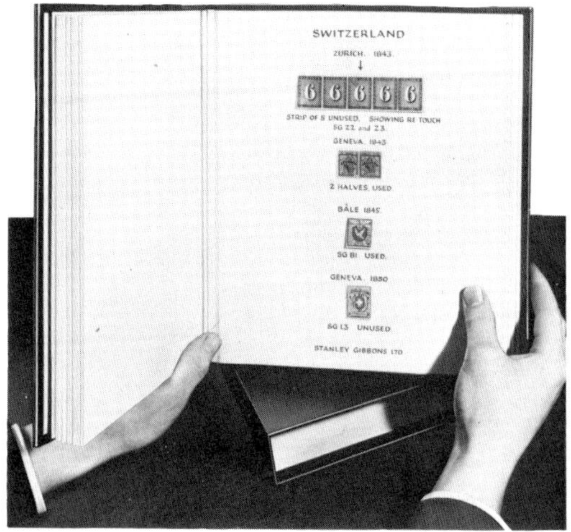

of the trade and his own very considerable resources in the lap of the potential investor, just as the stock-broker serves his clients.

The 'do-it-yourself' investor in stamps must rely on his own appraisal of the market and its fluctuations. The necessary intuition and an instinctive 'flair' in selecting the material most likely to appreciate in value can only be acquired by a close study of price trends over the years. Older stamps in short supply, stamps or countries which suddenly become 'fashionable' – these are the ones to watch. The old classics often show startling increases in price because in many instances there are so few of them, and the laws of supply and demand begin to operate.

In recent years virtually all the older British stamps have increased in price by leaps and bounds as everyone who keeps up to date with catalogue prices will know. Will the trend continue? That's for you to decide but, in bookmaker's language, it's a pretty safe bet.

Sometimes the market is upset by the speculator, the professional who buys enormous quantities of a particular current stamp in the hope of 'cornering' the market and making an eventual 'killing'. But sooner or later he is forced to sell – at prices people are willing to pay. And that's the time to buy!

Banknotes and Coins

Everyone is interested in money – none more so than the notaphilist or collector of banknotes. The hobby has close associations with philately, for the same firms which engrave and print the finest postage stamps, their artists and engravers, are also employed in the production of beautifully printed paper money. Many people now collect banknotes for their artistic designs alone, though until 1970 there were just a few dedicated collectors in a 'hobby without a name'.

In that year, Stanley Gibbons launched 'Notaphily', the 'new' hobby of collecting banknotes, with the formation of a new company, the publication of *Collect British Banknotes*, a priced catalogue of British Treasury and Bank of England notes, and a banknote album.

While, in Great Britain, paper money has existed since the reign of Charles I with notes being issued by many hundreds of private banks over the years, the first notes were issued about A.D. 650, and were in common use in China by A.D. 1000. It was Marco Polo who first brought news to the West of the use of paper money, after his visit to the court of the Great Khan, the Tartar emperor of China. Identical Ming notes, dated *circa* 1350 and in a 'monster' size of 12×9 inches, are available to collectors.

Mauritius 1847
The famous 2d blue
'Post Office' used –

1962	**£5,000**
1968	**£13,000**
1972	**£22,500**
1974	**£27,000**

A Ming note – greatly reduced in size

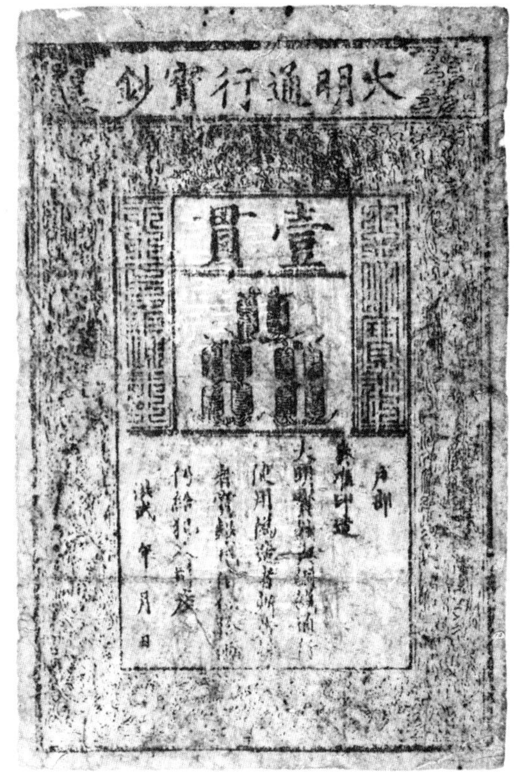

Many banknotes have designs in common with postage stamps, and in many instances stamps have been used as money by government authority: sometimes during emergencies, stamps have been printed on the backs of banknotes. The postal historian will find much to interest him in the events of the Boer War – Lord Baden-Powell designing emergency notes during the Siege of Mafeking, or in the American War of Independence, when Paul Revere, famous for his 'Midnight Ride', designed and printed notes for the American colonists.

The early colonial notes of America were hand-signed by many famous people and the development of the American dollar in world finance can make a rewarding banknote study.

The notes of Great Britain are of special interest. The Bank of England first issued notes in 1694, and to this day will redeem every note it ever issued – hence the expression 'as safe as the Bank of England'. There is also a large range of colourful notes of Scotland dating back to the 1690s, and there are several banks still issuing different notes there today.

Inexpensive collections can be formed with thematic interest, like the German 'Notgeld' – colourful emergency notes issued following World War I in many thousands of different designs. Some banknotes are as small as postage stamps, others are over a foot square, and many notaphilists collect 'one of each' of the different countries of the world.

The Gibbons's Banknote Album has a sprung-arch fitting with ten large PVC leaves, which hold four, three, two or one pockets in crystal-clear display, interleaved with fine white card. Extra leaves are available.

The collection and study of coins and medals – Numismatics, is a long-established hobby. Coined money originated probably in Lydia, where about 700 B.C. someone fashioned electrum, a mixture of gold and silver native to the country, into bean-shaped pieces of money. The new 'coinage' reached the mainland of Greece, and was thence quickly adopted by all the large trading-centres. Ancient coins give dates, names and places when other historical sources are missing.

Britain's gold sovereign, value one pound sterling, became the standard of British monetary value by the Coinage Act, 1816, and with the half-sovereign remained in use as everyday currency until 1914 when the Treasury issued £1 and 10s notes. They took their name from the head of the sovereign stamped upon them.

American Colonial Banknote

Charles II (1660–85) Gold Five Guineas 1668

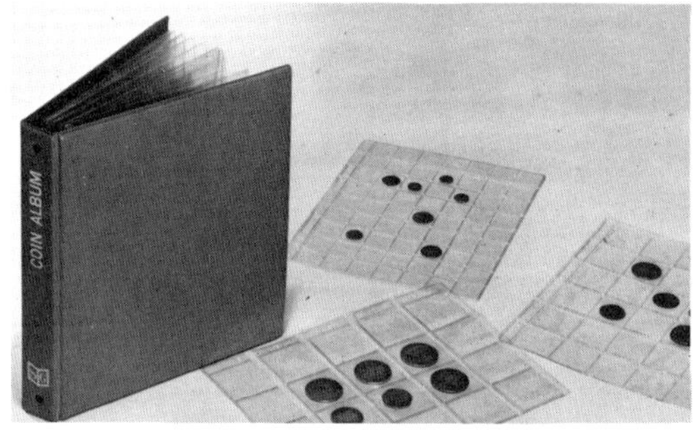

GLOSSARY OF TERMS AND INSCRIPTIONS

Adhesive A gummed stamp. In mint state, said to have its original gum ('O.G.')

Albino A design impression without colour

Aniline A fugitive ink or dye

Belgique-Belgie Belgium

Bisect A part of a stamp which has been cut in two or bisected for separate use

Block A group of four or more unseparated stamps

'Bradbury' Nickname for the first Treasury notes, signed by Sir John Bradbury

Cachet A commemorative inscription on a letter or postcard

Cancellation Any authorised defacing mark on a stamp

Centre The position of a stamp design within its perforations or margins

Ceskoslovensko Czechoslovakia

Charity stamp One bearing a premium for charitable purposes

Classic A country's early stamp issues up to about 1875; a choice stamp

Coil stamp One from a roll of stamps used in vending machines

Controls Letters/numerals appearing in the sheet margins of British stamps (discontinued in 1947)

Cover A postally used envelope, letter-sheet or wrapper

Cylinder number Number in sheet margin identifying printing cylinder used

Dandy roll Wire-mesh roller used in paper-making; the attached 'bits' provide the watermark emblems

Danmark Denmark

Die The original engraved plate from which printing plates for stamps and banknotes are prepared

Belgium

Bisect

Classic

Czechoslovakia

Stanley Gibbons
BLUE RIBAND APPROVALS

CAN HELP YOU TO BUILD YOUR COLLECTION INTO ONE OF YOUR PROUDEST POSSESSIONS

Write for full colour brochure:

**STANLEY GIBBONS
APPROVAL DEPARTMENT
391 STRAND
LONDON WC2R 0LX**

Embossing	A form of printing in relief
Entire	A *complete* envelope, letter-sheet or wrapper
Error	A mistake in stamp/banknote design, printing or production
España	Spain
Essay	A trial stamp/banknote design, differing from that issued
Face value	The denomination of a stamp, banknote or coin expressed on its face
Fiscal	A stamp used for revenue purposes
Helvetia	Switzerland
Imperforate	Stamps printed without perforations
Imprint	The name of the printer or issuing authority inscribed in the sheet margin
Iran	Persia
Island	Iceland
Liban	Lebanon
Local	A stamp with limited postal use and validity
'Machin'	The name given to current British definitive stamps bearing the Queen's head, designed by Arnold Machin
Magyar Posta	Hungary
Mint	A stamp, banknote or coin in its original pristine state
Nederland	Netherlands or Holland
Norge	Norway
Obsolete	A stamp, banknote or coin which is no longer in circulation
Obverse	The front of a banknote or coin
Overprint	A printed addition to a stamp or banknote
Pair	Two unseparated stamps, joined as originally issued
Pane	A divided part of a sheet of stamps; a leaf of four or six stamps in a stamp booklet
Perforations	Holes punched between stamps in sheets for ease in separation
Phosphor stamps	Overprinted, inked or impregnated with phosphorescent materials which 'fluoresce' in electronic letter-facing machines
Plate number	Number in sheet margin identifying printing plate used
Postmark	Any mark cancelling the stamp

Spain

Switzerland

Imprint

Iceland

Norway

and recording its passage through the mails

Proof A trial impression taken from a die or printing plate

Provisional A stamp, often overprinted or surcharged, issued for emergency or temporary use

Remainders Stamps remaining in official stocks after being declared obsolete

Reprint Stamps printed again after an original issue has been declared obsolete

Reverse The back of a banknote or coin

Specimen A sample stamp or banknote, usually with the word 'specimen' overprinted or perforated on it

Strip Three or more stamps joined in a row

Suomi Finland

Surcharge An overprint which specifically changes the face value of a stamp or banknote

Sverige Sweden

Tête-bêche A stamp inverted in relation to the adjoining stamp in a pair. Two *different* stamps in a joined pair are described as being *se-tenant* (i.e. joined together)

Unused An uncancelled stamp, not necessarily 'mint'

Used A stamp which has been postally used and has been appropriately postmarked

Used abroad Stamps of one country used and postmarked in another

Variety A stamp differing in some detail from the normal issue

Vignette The central portion of a stamp design, strictly one which shades off at its edges

Watermark A distinctive device or emblem in stamps and banknotes, formed by the deliberate 'thinning' of the paper during production

'Wilding' The name given to British definitive stamps issued between 1952 and about 1967, bearing the Queen's head from a portrait by Dorothy Wilding

Strip

Finland

Sweden

***Tête-bêche* 'Wilding' stamps**